James Joyce

The Works of
James Joyce

*with an Introduction by Michael Patrick Gillespie,
and Bibliography*

Wordsworth Poetry Library

This edition published 1995 by Wordsworth Editions Ltd,
Cumberland House, Crib Street, Ware, Hertfordshire SG12 9ET.

Copyright © Wordsworth Editions Ltd 1995.

All rights reserved. This publication may not be
reproduced, stored in a retrieval system,
or transmitted, in any form or by any means, electronic,
mechanical, photocopying, recording or otherwise,
without the prior permission of the publishers.

ISBN 1-85326-427-X

Typeset in the UK by Antony Gray.
Printed and bound in Denmark by Nørhaven.

The paper in this book is produced from pure wood
pulp, without the use of chlorine or any other substance
harmful to the environment. The energy used in its
production consists almost entirely of hydroelectricity
and heat generated from waste materials, thereby
conserving fossil fuels and contributing little to the
greenhouse effect.

INTRODUCTION

Throughout his artistic life, James Joyce thought of himself as a poet, and the verses collected in this volume offer readers representative examples of his control of the genre in which he refined the lyrical power that has come to characterise all of his writing. The Wordsworth edition reprints Joyce's *Collected Poems*, a volume first published by The Black Sun Press in 1936 and then, a year later, by Viking Press of New York. It brings together two previously published books of poetry – *Chamber Music* (1907) and *Pomes Penyeach* (1927) – and 'Ecce Puer', a poem written by Joyce in 1932.

Chamber Music, Joyce's first book to appear in print, was brought out in May 1907 in London by Elkin Mathews. It contains thirty-six related poems charting in a lyrical tone the diverse feelings inspired by an idealised love that ends in failure. The ordering of these Elizabethan-like songs expresses a tonality of varied emotions through vivid, sensuous imagery and exuberant, evocative symbolism. The change of seasons, the passing of day into night, the presence of a portentous moon, the flight of a bat, the imagery of water and birds, the mixture of colour, sound, time, and place, among many other images and symbols, all contribute to the atmosphere and shifting moods Joyce creates in this suite of songs.

Its highly personal form draws its emotional tenor from feelings shaping Joyce's temperament from 1901 through 1904 – the period of the poems' composition – and this group of poems introduces many of the themes that will come to dominate his subsequent work: the allurement and frustrations of love, the bitterness and desolation that come out of feelings of betrayal, rejection, loneliness, social censure, the complex function of art within the human consciousness, and the contrasting public and private roles of a poet.

Evidence from Joyce's letters indicates that he originally intended a two-part arrangement of the poems, portraying the rise and fall of consummated love. He also hoped that the poems might eventually be set to music. In 1907, the year *Chamber Music* was first published, G. Molyneux Palmer wrote to Joyce asking permission to do just that for a few of the poems, and he was given Joyce's whole-hearted encouragement. By 1909, Joyce had received copies of several of the poems that Palmer had set to music, and in a July 1909 letter he urged the composer to expand his project, saying, 'I hope you may set all of *Chamber Music* in time. This was indeed partly my idea in writing it. The book is in fact a suite of songs and if I were a musician I suppose I should have set them to music myself. The central song is xiv after which the movement is all downwards until xxxiv which is vitally the end of the book. xxxv and xxxvi are tailpieces just as i and iii are preludes' (*Letters*, i. 67). Although Palmer was one of the first composers to prepare arrangements for the poems, it was Adolf Mann's setting of 'Donnycarney' (xxxi) that first reached a public audience in 1910.

Despite the extensive work that Palmer did on the poems, now documented by Myra Russel, the significance of the collection rests upon the verse itself. Several of the poems of this collection have been anthologised, and one of the best known is the final selection, xxxvi. It was reprinted by Ezra Pound in 1914 in his *Des Imagistes* anthology under the title 'I Hear an Army', and its striking tone sets it off from others in the collection and evokes the Imagist tone of Pound's 'make it new' credo. It also served to introduce Joyce and Pound, and thus to initiate an association between the two men that would lead to Pound's energetic promotion of Joyce's work – principally *Dubliners*, *A Portrait of the Artist as a Young Man* and *Ulysses* – for the next decade.

The title *Chamber Music* was not preferred by Joyce, and he voiced his dissatisfaction in a letter to his brother, Stanislaus Joyce, in the fall of 1906: 'The reason I dislike *Chamber Music* as a title is that it is too complacent. I should prefer a title which to a certain extent repudiated the book, without altogether disparaging it' (*Letters*, ii. 182). What he actually meant by this is not altogether certain, but his intention seems clearer in a later correspondence with his brother in March 1907, when Joyce had just received the proofs of the book: 'I don't like the book but wish it were published and be damned to it. However, it is a young man's book. I felt like that. It is not a book of love-verses at all, I perceive' (Letters, ii. 219). Although there are varying accounts of the title's origin, the author's brother Stanislaus is purportedly the originator of it: 'I had already suggested,' Stanislaus writes in *My Brother's Keeper*, 'and Jim had accepted the title *Chamber Music* for the collection.'*

Pomes Penyeach, on the other hand, stands as a far less unified effort. It is

* 'Another version of the origin of the title is given in Herbert Gorman's biography of my brother, but the story there told . . . is false, whatever its source' (pp. 209–10). In the version of the story recounted by Herbert Gorman, Joyce and a friend visit a widow who, after hearing Joyce's poems and drinking beer, withdraws behind a screen to use a chamber pot. Although out of sight, she could be heard as

in fact a collection of thirteen poems on disparate but generally personal topics written by Joyce. He composed the bulk of these verses in Trieste between 1913 and 1915, during the time that he was completing *A Portrait of the Artist as a Young Man*, writing his play *Exiles* and beginning work on *Ulysses*. None the less, some, like 'Tilly' written in its earliest form in 1903, retain the traces of Joyce's very early poetic efforts, while others were written later in Zurich, between 1915 and 1919, and even, in the case of 'A Prayer', in Paris in the spring of 1924. Shakespeare and Company, the bookshop owned by Sylvia Beach, published the collection in mid-1927.

Many of the works in this collection reflect their status as occasional pieces, and as such they preserve notable moments in Joyce's personal and in his artistic development. 'Watching the Needleboats at San Sabba', for example, commemorates Joyce's viewing a competition of racing shells in which Joyce's brother, Stanislaus, participated. 'A Flower Given to My Daughter' recollects and idealises the kindness of a young woman to Lucia Joyce. 'She Weeps over Rahoon' retells the story of the youthful infatuation in Galway of Michael Bodkin with Nora Barnacle (who would later become Joyce's wife), earlier fictionalised in the *Dubliners* short story, 'The Dead'. The poem 'On the Beach at Fontana', on the other hand, attempts to capture a father's feelings while bathing with his son.

Pomes Penyeach stands in sharp contrast to the early versions of *Finnegans Wake* that were appearing in journals like *Transition*, the *Transatlantic Review* and *Navire d'Argent* at about the same time. None the less, despite its markedly different form, the collection offers important insights into Joyce's artistic consciousness. During a period when he has undertaken a radical reconfiguration of the protocols of prose fiction, he shows himself simultaneously disposed to write and to publish verse in what by contrast is a most conventional form. One gesture does not negate the other but rather each informs our sense of the scope of his creative dimensions.

The final work in this collection, 'Ecce Puer', was published in the January 1933 issue of *The Criterion* and appeared four years later in *Collected Poems*. It reflects the work of an artist far more mature than the author of *Chamber Music*, exploring contrasting emotions of joy and sorrow by juxtaposing Joyce's responses to watershed events in his life. 'Ecce Puer'

---

she urinated. ' "By God!" [Joyce's friend] cried, "she's a critic!" ' (Gorman, *James Joyce*, p. 154). The chamber-pot account reappears in *Ulysses* when Leopold Bloom offers a practical reason for such a title: 'Chamber Music. Could make a kind of pun on that' (*Ulysses*, 11: 979–80).

celebrates the birth of his grandson, Stephen James Joyce (15 February 1932), even as it mourns the death of Joyce's father, John Stanislaus Joyce (29 December 1931).

The poem is made up of four stanzas of four lines each with the even-numbered lines set in paired rhymes. Throughout the first three stanzas the first two lines examine the joy that the birth of his grandson has brought Joyce while the last two lines explore the pain that he feels over the death of his father. The final stanza foregrounds a *cri de coeur* as the speaker exclaims

> O, father forsaken,
> Forgive your son!

With a writer of Joyce's stature, the temptation arises to judge all of his work against his greatest achievements: *Dubliners*, *A Portrait of the Artist as a Young Man*, *Ulysses* and *Finnegans Wake*. In this case, however, such an analogy misses the point. Joyce's poetry develops according to the conventions of a genre completely different from those of fiction, yet it none the less demonstrates the creative power of one of the twentieth century's greatest writers.

Michael Patrick Gillespie
Marquette University

FURTHER READING

Boyle, Robert, S.J., 'The Woman in *Chamber Music*', in *Women and Joyce*, eds Suzette Henke and Elaine Unkeless, Urbana: University of Illinois Press, 1982

Ellmann, Richard, *James Joyce*, New York: Oxford University Press, 1982

Gorman, Herbert S., *James Joyce: A Definitive Biography*, 1941; reprinted London: John Lane, The Bodley Head, 1949

Joyce, James, *Letters of James Joyce*, Vol 1, ed. Stuart Gilbert, New York: Viking Press, 1957; reissued with corrections 1966. Vols II and III, ed. Richard Ellmann, New York: Viking Press, 1966

Russel, Myra Teicher (ed.), *James Joyce's Chamber Music: The Lost Settings*, Bloomington and Indianapolis: Indiana University Press, 1993

Scholes, Robert. 'James Joyce, Irish Poet', in *James Joyce Quarterly*, 4 (Summer 1965), pp. 255-70

CONTENTS

CHAMBER MUSIC

CHAMBER MUSIC

I

Strings in the earth and air
    Make music sweet;
Strings by the river where
    The willows meet.

There's music along the river
    For Love wanders there,
Pale flowers on his mantle,
    Dark leaves on his hair.

All softly playing,
    With head to the music bent,
And fingers straying
    Upon an instrument.

II

The twilight turns from amethyst
   To deep and deeper blue,
The lamp fills with a pale green glow
   The trees of the avenue.

The old piano plays an air,
   Sedate and slow and gay;
She bends upon the yellow keys,
   Her head inclines this way.

Shy thoughts and grave wide eyes and hands
   That wander as they list –
The twilight turns to darker blue
   With lights of amethyst.

III

At that hour when all things have repose,
   O lonely watcher of the skies,
    Do you hear the night wind and the sighs
Of harps playing unto Love to unclose
   The pale gates of sunrise?

When all things repose do you alone
   Awake to hear the sweet harps play
    To Love before him on his way,
And the night wind answering in antiphon
   Till night is overgone?

Play on, invisible harps, unto Love,
   Whose way in heaven is aglow
    At that hour when soft lights come and go,
Soft sweet music in the air above
   And in the earth below.

IV

When the shy star goes forth in heaven
    All maidenly, disconsolate,
Hear you amid the drowsy even
    One who is singing by your gate.
His song is softer than the dew
    And he is come to visit you.

O bend no more in revery
    When he at eventide is calling,
Nor muse: Who may this singer be
    Whose song about my heart is falling?
Know you by this, the lover's chant,
    'Tis I that am your visitant.

V

Lean out of the window,
    Goldenhair,
I heard you singing
    A merry air.

My book was closed;
    I read no more,
Watching the fire dance
    On the floor.

I have left my book,
    I have left my room,
For I heard you singing
    Through the gloom.

Singing and singing
    A merry air,
Lean out of the window,
    Goldenhair.

VI

I would in that sweet bosom be
   (O sweet it is and fair it is!)
Where no rude wind might visit me.
   Because of sad austerities
I would in that sweet bosom be.

I would be ever in that heart
   (O soft I knock and soft entreat her!)
Where only peace might be my part.
   Austerities were all the sweeter
So I were ever in that heart.

VII

My love is in a light attire
   Among the apple-trees,
Where the gay winds do most desire
   To run in companies.

There, where the gay winds stay to woo
   The young leaves as they pass,
My love goes slowly, bending to
   Her shadow on the grass;

And where the sky's a pale blue cup
   Over the laughing land,
My love goes lightly, holding up
   Her dress with dainty hand.

VIII

Who goes amid the green wood
   With springtide all adorning her?
Who goes amid the merry green wood
   To make it merrier?

Who passes in the sunlight
   By ways that know the light footfall?
Who passes in the sweet sunlight
   With mien so virginal?

The ways of all the woodland
   Gleam with a soft and golden fire –
For whom does all the sunny woodland
   Carry so brave attire?

O, it is for my true love
   The woods their rich apparel wear –
O, it is for my own true love,
   That is so young and fair.

IX

Winds of May, that dance on the sea,
Dancing a ring-around in glee
From furrow to furrow, while overhead
The foam flies up to be garlanded,
In silvery arches spanning the air,
Saw you my true love anywhere?
    Welladay! Welladay!
    For the winds of May!
Love is unhappy when love is away!

X

Bright cap and streamers,
   He sings in the hollow:
   Come follow, come follow,
     All you that love.
Leave dreams to the dreamers
   That will not after,
   That song and laughter
     Do nothing move.

With ribbons streaming
   He sings the bolder;
   In troop at his shoulder
     The wild bees hum.
And the time of dreaming
   Dreams is over –
   As lover to lover,
     Sweetheart, I come.

XI

Bid adieu, adieu, adieu,
   Bid adieu to girlish days,
Happy Love is come to woo
   Thee and woo thy girlish ways –
The zone that doth become thee fair,
The snood upon thy yellow hair.

When thou hast heard his name upon
   The bugles of the cherubim
Begin thou softly to unzone
   Thy girlish bosom unto him
And softly to undo the snood
That is the sign of maidenhood.

XII

What counsel has the hooded moon
   Put in thy heart, my shyly sweet,
Of Love in ancient plenilune,
   Glory and stars beneath his feet –
A sage that is but kith and kin
With the comedian Capuchin?

Believe me rather that am wise
   In disregard of the divine,
A glory kindles in those eyes,
   Trembles to starlight. Mine, O Mine!
No more be tears in moon or mist
For thee, sweet sentimentalist.

XIII

Go seek her out all courteously,
   And say I come,
Wind of spices whose song is ever
   Epithalamium.
O, hurry over the dark lands
   And run upon the sea
For seas and land shall not divide us
   My love and me.

Now, wind, of your good courtesy
   I pray you go,
And come into her little garden
   And sing at her window;
Singing: The bridal wind is blowing
   For Love is at his noon;
And soon will your true love be with you,
   Soon, O soon.

XIV

My dove, my beautiful one,
   Arise, arise!
   The night-dew lies
Upon my lips and eyes.

The odorous winds are weaving
   A music of sighs:
   Arise, arise,
My dove, my beautiful one!

I wait by the cedar tree,
   My sister, my love.
   White breast of the dove,
My breast shall be your bed.

The pale dew lies
   Like a veil on my head.
   My fair one, my fair dove,
Arise, arise!

XV

From dewy dreams, my soul, arise,
   From love's deep slumber and from death,
For lo! the trees are full of sighs
   Whose leaves the morn admonisheth.

Eastward the gradual dawn prevails
   Where softly-burning fires appear,
Making to tremble all those veils
   Of grey and golden gossamer.

While sweetly, gently, secretly,
   The flowery bells of morn are stirred
And the wise choirs of faery
   Begin (innumerous!) to be heard.

XVI

O cool is the valley now
   And there, love, will we go
For many a choir is singing now
   Where Love did sometime go.
And hear you not the thrushes calling,
   Calling us away?
O cool and pleasant is the valley
   And there, love, will we stay.

XVII

Because your voice was at my side
   I gave him pain,
Because within my hand I held
   Your hand again.

There is no word nor any sign
   Can make amend –
He is a stranger to me now
   Who was my friend.

XVIII

O Sweetheart, hear you
   Your lover's tale;
A man shall have sorrow
   When friends him fail.

For he shall know then
   Friends be untrue
And a little ashes
   Their words come to.

But one unto him
   Will softly move
And softly woo him
   In ways of love.

His hand is under
   Her smooth round breast;
So he who has sorrow
   Shall have rest.

XIX

Be not sad because all men
    Prefer a lying clamour before you:
Sweetheart, be at peace again –
    Can they dishonour you?

They are sadder than all tears;
    Their lives ascend as a continual sigh.
Proudly answer to their tears:
    As they deny, deny.

XX

In the dark pine-wood
   I would we lay,
In deep cool shadow
   At noon of day.

How sweet to lie there,
   Sweet to kiss,
Where the great pine-forest
   Enaisled is!

Thy kiss descending
   Sweeter were
With a soft tumult
   Of thy hair.

O, unto the pine-wood
   At noon of day
Come with me now,
   Sweet love, away.

XXI

He who hath glory lost, nor hath
    Found any soul to fellow his,
Among his foes in scorn and wrath
    Holding to ancient nobleness,
That high unconsortable one –
His love is his companion.

XXII

Of that so sweet imprisonment
    My soul, dearest, is fain —
Soft arms that woo me to relent
    And woo me to detain.
Ah, could they ever hold me there
Gladly were I a prisoner!

Dearest, through interwoven arms
    By love made tremulous,
That night allures me where alarms
    Nowise may trouble us;
But sleep to dreamier sleep be wed
Where soul with soul lies prisoned.

XXIII

This heart that flutters near my heart
   My hope and all my riches is,
Unhappy when we draw apart
   And happy between kiss and kiss;
My hope and all my riches – yes! –
And all my happiness.

For there, as in some mossy nest
   The wrens will divers treasures keep,
I laid those treasures I possessed
   Ere that mine eyes had learned to weep.
Shall we not be as wise as they
Though love live but a day?

XXIV

Silently she's combing,
   Combing her long hair,
Silently and graciously,
   With many a pretty air.

The sun is in the willow leaves
   And on the dappled grass,
And still she's combing her long hair
   Before the looking-glass.

I pray you, cease to comb out,
   Comb out your long hair,
For I have heard of witchery
   Under a pretty air,

That makes as one thing to the lover
   Staying and going hence,
All fair, with many a pretty air
   And many a negligence.

XXV

Lightly come or lightly go:
   Though thy heart presage thee woe,
Vales and many a wasted sun,
   Oread, let thy laughter run,
Till the irreverent mountain air
Ripple all thy flying hair.

Lightly, lightly – ever so:
   Clouds that wrap the vales below
At the hour of evenstar
   Lowliest attendants are;
Love and laughter song-confessed
When the heart is heaviest.

XXVI

Thou leanest to the shell of night,
   Dear lady, a divining ear.
In that soft choiring of delight
   What sound hath made thy heart to fear?
Seemed it of rivers rushing forth
From the grey deserts of the north?

   That mood of thine, O timorous,
Is his, if thou but scan it well,
   Who a mad tale bequeaths to us
At ghosting hour conjurable –
    And all for some strange name he read
    In Purchas or in Holinshed.

XXVII

Though I thy Mithridates were,
    Framed to defy the poison-dart,
Yet must thou fold me unaware
    To know the rapture of thy heart,
And I but render and confess
The malice of thy tenderness.

For elegant and antique phrase,
    Dearest, my lips wax all too wise;
Nor have I known a love whose praise
    Our piping poets solemnize,
Neither a love where may not be
Ever so little falsity.

XXVIII

Gentle lady, do not sing
   Sad songs about the end of love;
Lay aside sadness and sing
   How love that passes is enough.

Sing about the long deep sleep
   Of lovers that are dead, and how
In the grave all love shall sleep:
   Love is aweary now.

XXIX

Dear heart, why will you use me so?
　　Dear eyes that gently me upbraid,
Still are you beautiful – but O,
　　How is your beauty raimented!

Through the clear mirror of your eyes,
　　Through the soft cry of kiss to kiss,
Desolate winds assail with cries
　　The shadowy garden where love is.

And soon shall love dissolved be
　　When over us the wild winds blow –
But you, dear love, too dear to me,
　　Alas! why will you use me so?

XXX

Love came to us in time gone by
    When one at twilight shyly played
And one in fear was standing nigh –
    For Love at first is all afraid.

We were grave lovers. Love is past
    That had his sweet hours many a one;
Welcome to us now at the last
    The ways that we shall go upon.

XXXI

O, it was out by Donnycarney
  When the bat flew from tree to tree
My love and I did walk together;
  And sweet were the words she said to me.

Along with us the summer wind
  Went murmuring – O, happily! –
But softer than the breath of summer
  Was the kiss she gave to me.

XXXII

Rain has fallen all the day.
   O come among the laden trees:
The leaves lie thick upon the way
   Of memories.

Staying a little by the way
   Of memories shall we depart.
Come, my beloved, where I may
   Speak to your heart.

XXXIII

Now, O now, in this brown land
   Where Love did so sweet music make
We two shall wander, hand in hand,
   Forbearing for old friendship' sake,
Nor grieve because our love was gay
Which now is ended in this way.

A rogue in red and yellow dress
   Is knocking, knocking at the tree;
And all around our loneliness
   The wind is whistling merrily.
The leaves – they do not sigh at all
When the year takes them in the fall.

Now, O now, we hear no more
   The villanelle and roundelay!
Yet will we kiss, sweetheart, before
   We take sad leave at close of day.
Grieve not, sweetheart, for anything –
The year, the year is gathering.

XXXIV

Sleep now, O sleep now,
   O you unquiet heart!
A voice crying "Sleep now"
   Is heard in my heart.

The voice of the winter
   Is heard at the door.
O sleep, for the winter
   Is crying "Sleep no more."

My kiss will give peace now
   And quiet to your heart –
Sleep on in peace now,
   O you unquiet heart!

XXXIII

All day I hear the noise of waters
    Making moan,
Sad as the sea-bird is, when going
    Forth alone,
He hears the winds cry to the waters'
    Monotone.

The grey winds, the cold winds are blowing
    Where I go.
I hear the noise of many waters
    Far below.
All day, all night, I hear them flowing
    To and fro.

XXXVI

I hear an army charging upon the land,
   And the thunder of horses plunging, foam about their
      knees:
Arrogant, in black armour, behind them stand,
   Disdaining the reins, with fluttering whips, the
      charioteers.

They cry unto the night their battle-name:
   I moan in sleep when I hear afar their whirling
      laughter.
They cleave the gloom of dreams, a blinding flame,
   Clanging, clanging upon the heart as upon an anvil.

They come shaking in triumph their long, green hair:
   They come out of the sea and run shouting by the
      shore.
My heart, have you no wisdom thus to despair?
   My love, my love, my love, why have you left me
      alone?

POMES PENYEACH

Tilly

He travels after a winter sun,
Urging the cattle along a cold red road,
Calling to them, a voice they know,
He drives his beasts above Cabra.

The voice tells them home is warm.
They moo and make brute music with their hoofs.
He drives them with a flowering branch before him,
Smoke pluming their foreheads.

Boor, bond of the herd,
Tonight stretch full by the fire!
I bleed by the black stream
For my torn bough!

Watching the Needleboats at San Sabba

I heard their young hearts crying
Loveward above the glancing oar
And heard the prairie grasses sighing:
No more, return no more!

O hearts, O sighing grasses,
Vainly your loveblown bannerets mourn!
No more will the wild wind that passes
Return, no more return.

A Flower Given to my Daughter

Frail the white rose and frail are
Her hands that gave
Whose soul is sere and paler
Than time's wan wave.

Rosefrail and fair – yet frailest
A wonder wild
In gentle eyes thou veilest,
My blueveined child.

She Weeps over Rahoon

Rain on Rahoon falls softly, softly falling,
Where my dark lover lies.
Sad is his voice that calls me, sadly calling,
At grey moonrise.

Love, hear thou
How soft, how sad his voice is ever calling,
Ever unanswered and the dark rain falling,
Then as now.

Dark too our hearts, O love, shall lie and cold
As his sad heart has lain
Under the moongrey nettles, the black mould
And muttering rain.

Tutto è Sciolto

A birdless heaven, seadusk, one lone star
Piercing the west,
As thou, fond heart, love's time, so faint, so far,
Rememberest.

The clear young eyes' soft look, the candid brow,
The fragrant hair,
Falling as through the silence falleth now
Dusk of the air.

Why then, remembering those shy
Sweet lures, repine
When the dear love she yielded with a sigh
Was all but thine?

On the Beach at Fontana

Wind whines and whines the shingle,
The crazy pierstakes groan;
A senile sea numbers each single
Slimesilvered stone.

From whining wind and colder
Grey sea I wrap him warm
And touch his trembling fineboned shoulder
And boyish arm.

Around us fear, descending
Darkness of fear above
And in my heart how deep unending
Ache of love!

Simples

O bella bionda,
Sei come l'onda!

Of cool sweet dew and radiance mild
The moon a web of silence weaves
In the still garden where a child
Gathers the simple salad leaves.

A moondew stars her hanging hair
And moonlight kisses her young brow
And, gathering, she sings an air:
Fair as the wave is, fair, art thou!

Be mine, I pray, a waxen ear
To shield me from her childish croon
And mine a shielded heart for her
Who gathers simples of the moon.

Flood

Goldbrown upon the sated flood
The rockvine clusters lift and sway.
Vast wings above the lambent waters brood
Of sullen day.

A waste of waters ruthlessly
Sways and uplifts its weedy mane
Where brooding day stares down upon the sea
In dull disdain.

Uplift and sway, O golden vine,
Your clustered fruits to love's full flood,
Lambent and vast and ruthless as is thine
Incertitude!

Nightpiece

Gaunt in gloom,
The pale stars their torches,
Enshrouded, wave.
Ghostfires from heaven's far verges faint illume,
Arches on soaring arches,
Night's sindark nave.

Seraphim,
The lost hosts awaken
To service till
In moonless gloom each lapses muted, dim,
Raised when she has and shaken
Her thurible.

And long and loud,
To night's nave upsoaring,
A starknell tolls
As the bleak incense surges, cloud on cloud,
Voidward from the adoring
Waste of souls.

Alone

The moon's greygolden meshes make
All night a veil,
The shorelamps in the sleeping lake
Laburnum tendrils trail.

The sly reeds whisper to the night
A name – her name –
And all my soul is a delight,
A swoon of shame.

A Memory of the Players
in a Mirror at Midnight

They mouth love's language. Gnash
The thirteen teeth
Your lean jaws grin with. Lash
Your itch and quailing, nude greed of the flesh.
Love's breath in you is stale, worded or sung,
As sour as cat's breath,
Harsh of tongue.

This grey that stares
Lies not, stark skin and bone.
Leave greasy lips their kissing. None
Will choose her what you see to mouth upon.
Dire hunger holds his hour.
Pluck forth your heart, saltblood, a fruit of tears.
Pluck and devour!

Bahnhofstrasse

The eyes that mock me sign the way
Whereto I pass at eve of day,

Grey way whose violet signals are
The trysting and the twining star.

Ah star of evil! star of pain!
Highhearted youth comes not again

Nor old heart's wisdom yet to know
The signs that mock me as I go.

A Prayer

Again!
Come, give, yield all your strength to me!
From far a low word breathes on the breaking brain
Its cruel calm, submission's misery,
Gentling her awe as to a soul predestined.
Cease, silent love! My doom!

Blind me with your dark nearness, O have mercy,
    beloved enemy of my will!
I dare not withstand the cold touch that I dread.
Draw from me still
My slow life! Bend deeper on me, threatening head,
Proud by my downfall, remembering, pitying
Him who is, him who was!

Again!
Together, folded by the night, they lay on earth. I hear
From far her low word breathe on my breaking brain.
Come! I yield. Bend deeper upon me! I am here.
Subduer, do not leave me! Only joy, only anguish,
Take me, save me, soothe me, O spare me!

Ecce Puer

Of the dark past
A child is born
With joy and grief
My heart is torn

Calm in his cradle
The living lies.
May love and mercy
Unclose his eyes!

Young life is breathed
On the glass;
The world that was not
Comes to pass.

A child is sleeping:
An old man gone.
O, father forsaken,
Forgive your son!

INDEX OF FIRST LINES

Now, O now, in this brown land 33

O cool is the valley now 16
O, it was out by Donnycarney 31
O Sweetheart, hear you 18
Of cool sweet dew and radiance mild 43
Of that so sweet imprisonment 22
Of the dark past 51

Rain has fallen all the day 32
Rain on Rahoon falls softly, softly falling 40

Silently she's combing 24
Sleep now, O sleep now 34
Strings in the earth and air 1

The eyes that mock me sign the way 48
The moon's greygolden meshes make 46
The twilight turns from amethyst 2
They mouth love's language. Gnash 47
This heart that flutters near my heart 23
Thou leanest to the shell of night 26
Though I thy Mithridates were 27

What counsel has the hooded moon 12
When the shy star goes forth in heaven 4
Who goes amid the green wood 8
Wind whines and whines the shingle 42
Winds of May, that dance on the sea 9